I Can Make

JEWELRY

Makerspace Projects

Emily Reid

WINDMILL BOOKS
New York

Published in 2016 by **Windmill Books**, an Imprint of Rosen Publishing
29 East 21st Street, New York, NY 10010

Developed and produced for Rosen by BlueAppleWorks Inc.

Creative Director: Melissa McClellan
Managing Editor for BlueAppleWorks: Melissa McClellan
Designer: T.J. Choleva
Photo Research: Jane Reid
Editor: Janice Dyer
Craft Artisans: Jerrie McClellan (p. 8, 10, 12, 20, 24, 28); Jane Yates (p. 14, 16, 18, 22, 30); Eva Challen (p. 26)

Photo Credits: cover background image, title page background oksana2010/Shutterstock; cover bottom
inset right, title page bottom right, p. 8 top Yevgen Glukhov/Shutterstock; cover center image, cover insets,
title page, TOC, p. 4 bottom, p. 5 third row left, p. 7, 8–9, 10–11, 12–13, 14–15, 16–17, 18–19, 20–21, 22–23, 24–25,
26–27, 28-29, 30 Austen Photography; p. 4 top tescha555/Thinkstock; p. 5 first row right Photka/Dreamstime;
p. 5 second row left Design56/Dreamstime; Kguzel/Dreamstime; p. 5 second row middle Gregd/Dreamstime;
p. 5 second row right Fuse/Thinkstock; Dreamstime; p. 5 third row middle Sergey Mostovoy/Dreamstime;
p. 5 third row right (left to right) Crackerclips/Dreamstime; Anphotos/Dreamstime; Jerryb8/Dreamstime;
p. 5 fourth row left (left to right) Andreja Donko/Dreamstime; azgek/Thinkstock; Stephanie Connell/
Dreamstime; p. 5 fourth row right (left to right clockwise) antpkr/Thinkstock; Arinahabich08/Dreamstime;
Gradts/Dreamstime; Onur Ersin/Dreamstime; sodapix sodapix/Thinkstock; p. 6 top, 25 top right Jakub
Krechowicz/Dreamstime; p. 6 middle Steveheap/Dreamstime; p. 9 top right Yarvet/Dreamstime; p. 11 top
right Mbolina/Dreamstime; p. 13 top right Gerald R. Ford Presidential Library/Public Domain; p. 17 top right
Felinda/Dreamstime; p. 21 top right Mariontxa/Shutterstock; p. 29 top right Rogers Fund, 1954/Jastrow/
Creative Commons.

Cataloging-in-Publication-Data
Reid, Emily.
I can make jewelry / by Emily Reid.
p. cm. — (Makerspace projects)
Includes index.
ISBN 978-1-4777-5641-6 (pbk.)
ISBN 978-1-4777-5640-9 (6-pack)
ISBN 978-1-4777-5564-8 (library binding)
1. Jewelry making — Juvenile literature.
2. Handicraft — Juvenile literature. I. Title.
TT171.R45 2016
745.594'2—d23

Manufactured in the United States of America
CPSIA Compliance Information: Batch #WS15WM: For Further Information contact: Rosen Publishing, New York, New York at 1-800-237-9932

CONTENTS

Materials	4
Techniques	6
Felt Pin	8
Clay Beads	10
Tiara	12
Necklace	14
Zipper Pull	16
Friendship Bracelet	18
Straw Beads	20
Barrette	22
Button Fun	24
Paracord Bracelet	26
Headband	28
Jewelry Box	30
Patterns	31
Glossary	32
For More Information	32
Index	32

MATERIALS

Make your own makerspace a place to create jewelry. You can dedicate a space for your makerspace, or make one as you need it. You may already have many of the basic supplies for your makerspace. You can purchase whatever else you need at a craft store or dollar store. If you don't have a dedicated area, make a portable makerspace by organizing your supplies in boxes or plastic bins and pull them out when you want to create.

AIR-DRYING CLAY

Air-drying clay is easy to use and best of all, doesn't need to be heated to dry. Most kinds dry in a day or two. Always make sure to wrap up what you haven't used in the wrapper it came in, or in a freezer bag if it is homemade, so it doesn't dry out.

Most air-drying clay comes in a variety of colors. If you only have white clay, add small amounts of acrylic or poster paint to the clay to color it or paint it when it is dry.

A note about patterns

Some of the jewelry projects in this book use patterns or **templates**. Trace the pattern, cut the pattern, and then place it on the material you want to cut out. You can either tape it in place and cut both the pattern and material, or trace around the pattern onto the material and then cut it out.

MAKE YOUR OWN!

Mix 4 cups of flour and 1 cup of salt in a large bowl. Add 1¾ cups of warm water to the flour/salt mixture. **Knead** the clay dough.

PINS, CLASPS, SNAP CLIPS

BRADS AND FASTENERS

PAINT

CRAFT THREAD & CORDS

BEADS

BUTTONS

SEQUINS AND JEWEL STICKERS

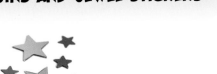

GLUE, TAPE, AND OTHER FASTENERS

PAPER AND FABRIC

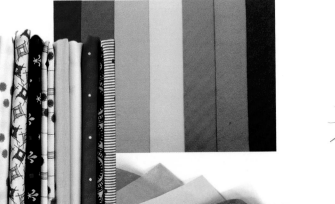

TOOLS

TECHNIQUES

Have fun while making your crafts. Be creative. Your project does not have to look just like the one in this book. If you don't have a certain material, think of something similar you could use. The following techniques will help you create your jewelry.

THREADING A NEEDLE

Threading a needle can be frustrating. The following tips will help.

- Cut more thread than you think you will need.
- Wet one end of the thread in your mouth.
- Poke it through the needle opening.
- Pull some of the thread through until you have an even amount and make a double knot.
- If you are using thicker thread like embroidery thread, do not double up the thread. Just pull a small amount through and make the knot at the other end.

EASIEST METHOD

- Use a metal needle threader.
- Push the metal threader through the needle hole, put the thread through the loop, and then pull the needle threader back through the needle.

Once the thread is in the loop, pull the loop back through the needle.

Put the thread through the loop.

BE SAFE

- Ask for help when you need it.
- Ask for permission to borrow tools from others.
- Be careful when using knives, scissors, and sewing needles.

BE PREPARED

- Read through the instructions and make sure you have all the materials you need.
- Cover your work area with newspaper or cardboard.
- Clean up your makerspace when you are finished making your project.

SEWING FABRIC

The whipstitch works great with felt. It is used to sew two pieces together.

- Place the needle and knotted thread in between the two pieces of felt and up through the top layer of felt.
- Take the needle behind both layers of felt at point 1.
- Pull the needle through both layers of felt at point 2.
- Continue stitching until finished.

1

2

USING COLLAGE

You can decorate your jewelry using the collage technique. Arrange and glue cut-up pieces of tissue paper, magazine pages or wrapping paper in an interesting pattern. You can also buy specialty glues which can be found in most crafting stores.

- Standard craft glue works best if it is diluted with a little water.
- Use a paintbrush to spread some of the glue onto a small part of your project. Press the paper into the glue.
- When you are finished gluing the paper, cover it with a thin layer of glue to seal the paper.
- Make sure to use glue that dries clear.

FASTENING NECKLACES AND BRACELETS

To tie the ends of a bracelet or necklace together use a double half-hitch knot.

- Take one end and make an underhand loop around the other end. Bring the same end up over the holding cord and through the eye which you created. Make a second underhand loop around the holding cord, and run the end through this eye. Pull tightly.

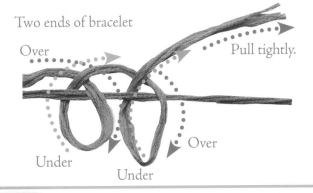

Two ends of bracelet

Over

Pull tightly.

Under

Over

Under

A note about measurements

Measurements are given in U.S. form with metric in brackets. The metric conversion is rounded to make it easier to measure.

Creating a craft from materials using your creativity is a very rewarding activity. When you are finished, you can say with great pride, **"I made that!"**

FELT PIN

You can make fun pins to wear or to decorate your backpack or coat. Felt pins also make a great gift!

You'll Need

- ✔ Tracing paper
- ✔ Pins
- ✔ Felt
- ✔ Scissors
- ✔ Pin back
- ✔ Needle
- ✔ Glue
- ✔ Embroidery thread
- ✔ Buttons

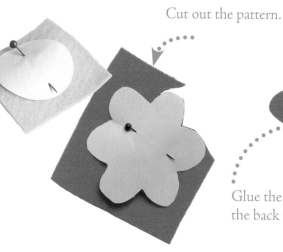

Cut out the pattern.

Pin the pattern to the felt.

Glue the pin back to the back of the felt.

1 Trace the pattern pieces on page 31 onto a piece of tracing paper. Trace an extra flower. Cut out the pieces.

2 Pin each pattern piece to your felt pieces. Using the pattern as a guide, cut out the felt pieces.

3 Sew or glue the pin back onto the back piece of the flower.

Attach the leaves to the front of the flower.

4 Sew or glue the leaves in place on the front edge of the flower.

5 Layer the front of the flower with a circle and large button and sew together through the button holes.

Sew the large button to the circle and flower.

6 Place the front and back together and sew using the technique described on page 7 along the edges.

Sew the front and back together.

Another Idea!

To make an owl or cat, follow steps 1 to 3 using the owl or cat pattern. Sew or glue the details on the front piece. For the owl, layer the front and back pieces with the feet between the layers and sew along the outside. For the cat, place a little bit of tissue paper between the front and back pieces to make the head puffy.

Tip When sewing, try to keep your stitches evenly spaced and the same size.

CLAY BEADS

Make your own clay beads with air-drying clay. You can make necklaces, earrings or bracelets with the beads!

You'll Need

✔ Air-drying clay
✔ Round toothpicks
✔ Needle
✔ Cord or elastic thread

Roll out two pieces of clay. Then twist them together.

Roll the clay into a shape.

1 **Knead** a handful of clay in two separate colors until it becomes soft.

2 Take a small amount of each (about the size of a pea). Roll each piece into a long shape. Twist the pieces together.

3 Roll the twisted clay into a shape. You could make it round or rectangular. The more you roll the piece of clay, the more marbled it gets. Repeat steps 2 and 3 until you have made as many beads as you want.

Poke a hole in the bead.

Did You Know?

Marbleize means to make something look like marble.

4 Wet the end of a toothpick in a dish of water. Slowly insert the toothpick through the bead using a twisting motion. Remove gently and reshape the bead a little if necessary. For small beads, use a pin.

String the beads onto elastic thread.

5 When the beads are dry, lace them onto an elastic thread. Tie the ends together with a double knot.

Tip

Make sure the beads are not touching each other while drying or they will stick together.

Another Idea!

To make earrings, string some beads onto some cord, knot one end, and tie the other end to an earring finding. A finding is the piece that holds the earring to the ear. Findings come in fish hooks for pierced ears and as clip-ons.

TIARA

Look like royalty while wearing your own tiara! Decorate it with jewels or stickers to add to the glamour.

You'll Need

- ✔ Paper for tracing
- ✔ Glitter card stock
- ✔ Tape
- ✔ Scissors
- ✔ Glue
- ✔ Jewel brads or rhinestone stickers
- ✔ Metal fasteners (3)

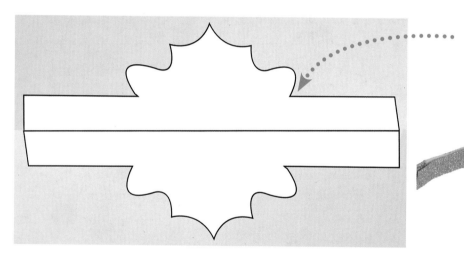

Cut along the edge of the pattern.

Glitter sides should both be on the outside.

1 Trace the pattern for the tiara from page 31 twice onto a piece of paper. Tape your patterns to the back of the card stock so that they mirror each other.

2 Cut out the tiara on the card stock using your pattern as a guide.

3 Fold the tiara in the middle.

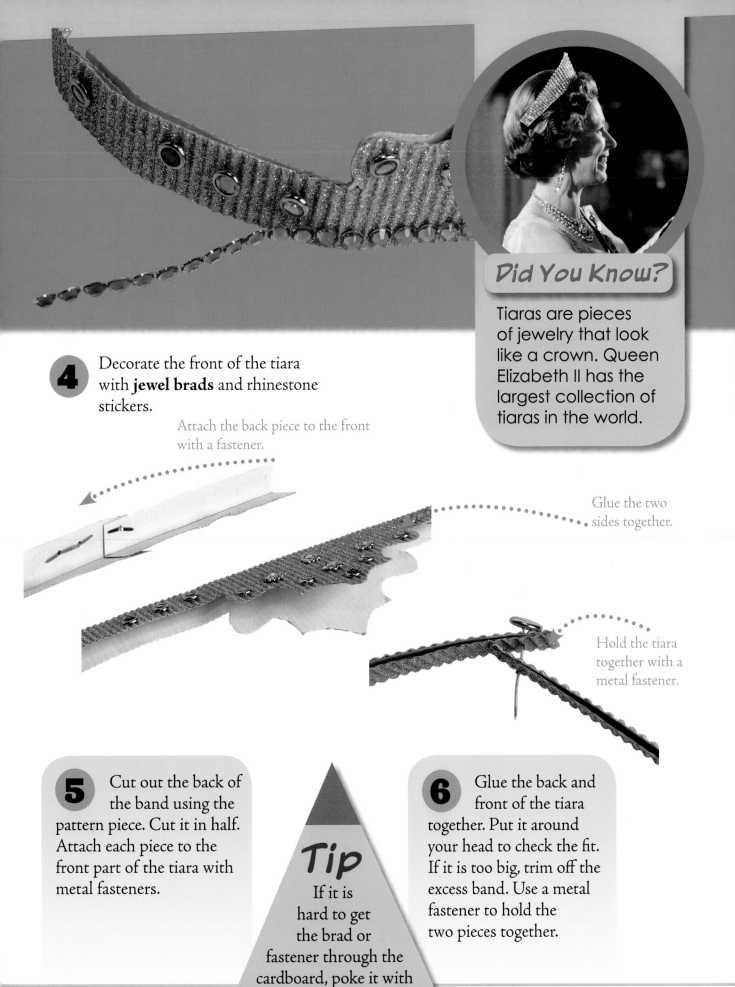

4 Decorate the front of the tiara with **jewel brads** and rhinestone stickers.

Attach the back piece to the front with a fastener.

Glue the two sides together.

Hold the tiara together with a metal fastener.

5 Cut out the back of the band using the pattern piece. Cut it in half. Attach each piece to the front part of the tiara with metal fasteners.

Tip
If it is hard to get the brad or fastener through the cardboard, poke it with a pin or needle first.

6 Glue the back and front of the tiara together. Put it around your head to check the fit. If it is too big, trim off the excess band. Use a metal fastener to hold the two pieces together.

NECKLACE

You can make great-looking necklaces with wood or glass beads. For extra pizzazz, add a pendant to the end of the necklace.

You'll Need

- ✔ Photo, sticker or magazine
- ✔ Circle punch (optional)
- ✔ Self-sealing laminated pouch (business card size)
- ✔ Craft wire
- ✔ Scissors
- ✔ Tape
- ✔ Beads
- ✔ Cord
- ✔ Clasp (optional)

Press the image in a self-sealing laminate pouch, then cut it out.

Attach a loop of wire or cord to the back of the photo.

1 To make the pendant, find an image that you like from a photo, sticker, or magazine. Use a circle punch to cut your image into a circle shape. or trace around the circle pattern found on page 31.

2 Place the image in a self-sealing laminate pouch. Press firmly to seal it. Cut around the image, leaving a border of laminate.

3 Make a small loop with craft wire or necklace cord. Tape the small loop to the back of your laminated image.

Place the pendant on the cord. Tie a knot on either side. Then string the beads.

4 Cut a piece of cord twice as long as you want your necklace to be. Place the pendant on the cord and slide it to the middle of the cord. Tie a knot on either side of the pendant.

5 String beads onto the cord. The number of beads will depend on how long you want the necklace. Tie a knot either between each bead or every three or four beads.

Tie

Clasp

6 Tie the two ends together and trim the extra.

Tip

You can buy wood or glass beads from a craft store or dollar store.

Another Idea!

If your necklace is short and will not fit over your head, tie each end to a necklace clasp so that you can open and close the necklace.

ZIPPER PULL

You can make cool zipper pulls to wear on your coat or to decorate your backpack.

You'll Need

- ✔ Bottle caps
- ✔ Hammer
- ✔ Nail
- ✔ Piece of wood
- ✔ Lanyard hook

- ✔ Photos, stickers or magazine
- ✔ 1 inch (2.5 cm) circle punch or scissors
- ✔ Clear glue

Flatten the bottle cap with a hammer.

Make a hole with a hammer and nail.

Put the hook through the hole.

1 Wash a bottle cap with soap and water. Dry it. Place the bottle cap on a piece of wood and carefully bang the edges of the cap with the hammer to flatten the bottle cap.

2 Keep the bottle cap on the piece of wood. Hammer a nail through the edge of the bottle cap. Repeat this process for as many caps as you want to make.

3 Remove the caps from the piece of wood. Put the lanyard hook through the hole.

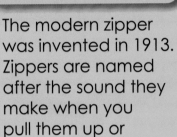

Did You Know?

The modern zipper was invented in 1913. Zippers are named after the sound they make when you pull them up or down—zip!

4 Gather the photos, stickers, or magazine cutouts you want to use. If you have a 1-inch (2.5 cm) circle punch, use it to cut your circles.

Glue the photo to the bottle cap.

Pour glue over the photo to protect it.

5 Place a small amount of glue on the back of your photo and then press it into the cap.

6 Pour a small amount of clear glue over the photo. Leave it to dry for a day.

Tip

If you don't have a circle punch, trace the pattern on page 31 of the circle. Place it over your photo and use it as a guide to cut out the photo.

Another Idea!

You can buy bottle caps with the hole already made or a metal loop already attached. If you do that you can skip the first two steps.

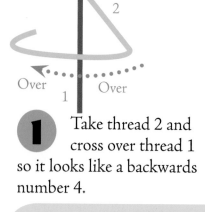

FRIENDSHIP BRACELET

Make a friendship bracelet and give it to someone as a symbol of your friendship. You can make one for yourself as well!

You'll Need

- ✔ Different colors of craft thread
- ✔ Scissors
- ✔ Beads
- ✔ Tape

Basic right-hand knot

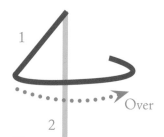

1 Take thread 1 and cross over thread 2 so it looks like a number 4.

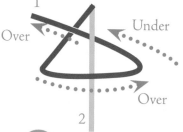

2 Take thread 1 and go under thread 2 and then back over thread 1.

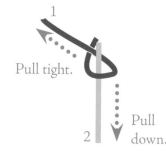

3 Pull thread 1 back to the left while pulling thread 2 toward you. Pull until it is tight.

Basic left-hand knot

1 Take thread 2 and cross over thread 1 so it looks like a backwards number 4.

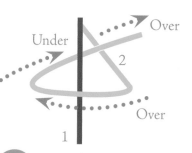

2 Take thread 2 and go under thread 1 and then back over thread 2.

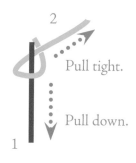

3 Pull thread 2 back to the right while pulling thread 1 toward you. Pull until it is tight.

To make a double knot, repeat the three steps.

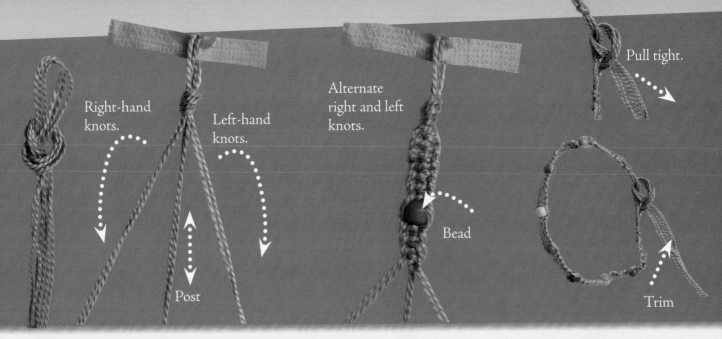

Right-hand knots.

Left-hand knots.

Post

Alternate right and left knots.

Bead

Pull tight.

Trim

How to make a ladder bracelet:

1 Start with three colors of craft thread, about 2 yards (about 2 m) each, folded in half. Tie a knot about ½ inch (1.3 cm) from the top. Secure the loop to the table with tape. Alternate right and left knots using the two outside colors.

2 To add beads to the bracelet, slide the bead on the middle thread (the post) and then continue with the next knot. Continue until the bracelet is long enough to go around your wrist.

3 Make a knot. Have a friend help you tie it around your wrist and trim the extra thread.

How to make a diagonal bracelet:

1 Start with four colors of craft thread, about 2 yards (about 2 m) each, folded in half. Tie a knot about ½ inch (1.3 cm) from the top. Secure the loop to the table with tape. Make sure all the colors are separate.

2 Make two right-hand knots starting with thread 1 and thread 2. Take thread 1 and make two right-hand knots with thread 3. Take thread 1 and make two right-hand knots with thread 4.

3 The first thread is now the fourth thread. Repeat step 2 with the second thread. Repeat step 2 with the third thread. Repeat step 2 with the fourth thread. Start again and repeat until you have a bracelet long enough to fit your wrist. Make a knot. Have a friend help you tie the bracelet around your wrist.

STRAW BEADS

You can make great looking beads with drinking straws and fabric. Use these beads to make beautiful bracelets or necklaces!

You'll Need

- ✔ Pencil
- ✔ Scissors
- ✔ Fabric
- ✔ Drinking straws
- ✔ Glue (white and clear)
- ✔ Brush
- ✔ Round elastic cord
- ✔ Washi tape (optional)

Roll the fabric around the straw.

1 Trace the triangle pattern found on page 31 onto a piece of paper. Cut the triangle out using scissors. Use this triangle as a guide for cutting out the fabric for the beads. You will need eight pieces to make a bracelet.

2 Cover the back of the fabric triangle with glue. Attach the wide end of the triangle to the straw and then roll the rest of the triangle around the straw.

3 Roll two more fabric triangles on the same straw. Repeat until you have rolled all eight fabric triangles.

4 Take a straw with beads on it and place a dab of glue on each bead. Using a small paintbrush, spread the glue around the outside of each bead. Place the straws in a glass to dry.

Did You Know?

Washi tape is a type of Japanese paper tape that comes in many pretty colors and patterns.

Tie

5 When the beads are dry, cut the straws at the edges of each bead. Lace the beads through 12 inches (30 cm) of elastic cord. Tie a double knot and cut off the extra cord with your scissors.

Tip
You can make the beads different sizes by making the triangle pattern smaller or bigger.

Another Idea!

You can use washi tape instead. Cut 2-inch (5 cm) pieces of tape and wrap them around the straw. Glue the end down to make sure it stays secure. Repeat. Cut the straw at the edges of the beads.

BARRETTE

Make your own barrettes and then use them to make cool hairstyles for you and your friends!

You'll Need

- Metal snap clips
- Lid (from used bottles)
- Craft glue
- Acrylic paint
- Stir stick
- Ribbon
- Beads
- Fabric
- Sequins
- Double-sided tape

To make a beaded barrette:

Mix the paint and glue.

Cover the clip with glue.

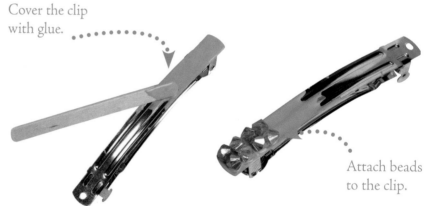

Attach beads to the clip.

1 Choose a metal snap clip to use. Pour some glue into a lid. Add a few drops of paint to color the glue.

2 Using a stir stick, cover the clip with glue. Cover a small amount at a time so it doesn't dry out while you're working.

3 Place beads on the glue. Add more glue as needed. Continue until the clip is covered in beads. Leave the finished barrette to dry for several hours so that the beads stay in place.

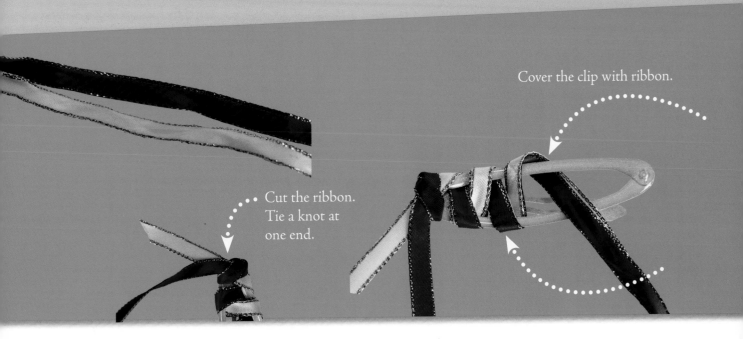

Cut the ribbon.
Tie a knot at
one end.

Cover the clip with ribbon.

To make a ribboned barrette:

1 Take two pieces of ribbon about 15 inches (38 cm) long. Put one on top of the other and make a knot. Put a small amount of glue on the tip of the barrette. Slip the knot over the top of the barrette and press down to hold it in place.

2 Slip the ribbon over one side of the barrette, under the other side, and then back over that side. Repeat until you have covered the barrette. When you come back, the other side of the ribbon should be showing.

Trim the ends of the ribbon.

3 When you get to the end, leave the two ribbons. Trim the ends. Put a small amount of glue on the barrette and press the ribbon to the glue to secure them.

Another Idea!

Cut out a piece of cardboard the same size as the barrette. Cover the cardboard in fabric and glue it in place. Tape the cardboard with double-sided tape to the barrette. Glue sequins on the front.

BUTTON FUN

You can make all kinds of jewelry with buttons, such as rings and bracelets. Use your imagination to create beautiful crafts with buttons!

You'll Need

- ✔ Buttons
- ✔ Elastic cord
- ✔ Scissors
- ✔ Ribbon
- ✔ Charm
- ✔ Chenille stems
- ✔ Air-drying clay

- ✔ Decorative object (rhinestone or gem sticker, bead, and sequin)

Thread the buttons on the pieces of cord.

Make a double knot.

Make a double knot.

Add a charm.

1 Choose about 50 small, pretty buttons. Measure elastic cord to fit around your wrist, add several extra inches and then cut the cord. Cut another piece the same size. String each cord through two of the openings in the buttons and tie a knot.

2 String more buttons through the two cords. String the buttons randomly or follow a pattern, such as two of one color then three of the next color. Keep adding buttons until you have enough to go around your wrist.

3 Tie the ends of the cords together and make a double knot. Trim off the extra cord. You can tie a charm to the end of the bracelet using ribbon to add a nice finishing touch.

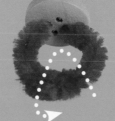

Thread the button onto the chenille stem.

Twist the ends of the chenille stem together.

Did You Know?

Many museums around the world have collections of buttons. In the past, buttons were used for decoration instead of to fasten things.

1 Choose a ring-sized button. Cut a 2- to 3-inch (5 to 7.5 cm) piece of chenille stem. Bend the chenille stem in half. Insert both ends through the holes in the button.

2 Twist the two ends of the chenille stem together. Fold in the metal tips. Make sure the chenille stem fits snugly around your finger.

How to make a button ring:

3 Cover the surface of the button with air-drying clay.

4 Time to decorate! Press rhinestones, stickers, beads, or sequins into the clay. Let the clay dry.

Another Idea!

Skip step 3 and instead glue a bead or other decoration directly to the button.

PARACORD BRACELET

Parachute cord bracelets are useful and attractive. Outdoor adventurers use them for safety. If you need a rope you just unravel the bracelet. Others wear them as an **accessory**!

You'll Need

- ✔ 6–7 feet (about 2 m) of paracord
- ✔ **Carabiner**
- ✔ Tape
- ✔ Scissors
- ✔ Clear glue

Cobra knot right side

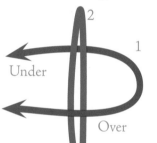

1 Take cord 1 and cross over cord 2 to make a loop on the right side of cord 2.

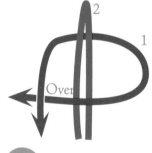

2 Take the top part of the loop and go over the bottom part of the loop.

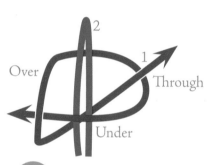

3 Continue with that section of cord and go under and through the loop. Then pull both parts of cord 1 tight.

Cobra knot left side

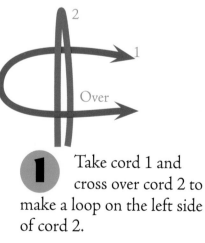

1 Take cord 1 and cross over cord 2 to make a loop on the left side of cord 2.

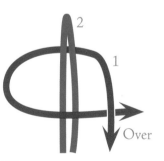

2 Take the top part of the loop and go over the bottom part of the loop.

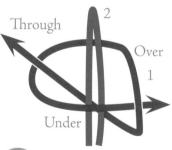

3 Continue with that section of cord and go under and through the loop. Pull both parts of cord 1 tight.

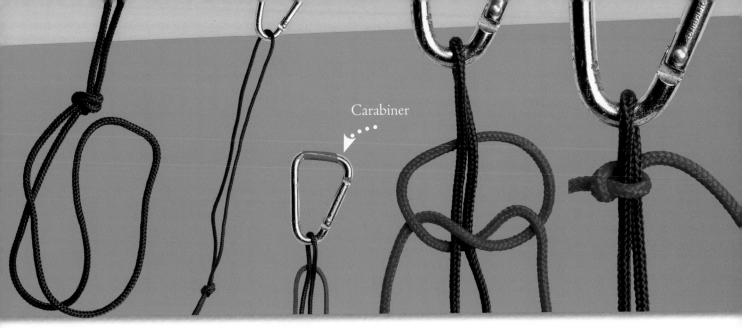

Carabiner

1 Make the core loop first. Wrap the end of the cord around your wrist three times and then cut the cord. Unfold the cord and then fold it in half. Make a knot at the open end. Put it over your wrist and adjust the knot until it fits loose enough to fit a couple of fingers between the cord and your wrist.

2 Put the end of the loop through a carabiner and tape it to a table. It will make it easier if you tape the bottom knot to the table as well. Prepare the cord. You will need at least 5 to 6 feet (about 1.5 m) of cord. Hold both ends together to find the center. Place the center under the loop about ½ inch (1.3 cm) from the end.

3 Make a right side cobra knot. Then make a left side cobra knot. Alternate the knots until you get close to the knot at the other end of the loop. If you forget which knot you made last, the loop goes on the side with the knot.

Through

Under

Under

Make the loop on the side with the knot.

4 When you are very close to the bottom knot, turn the bracelet over. Tuck both ends of the cord under the last knot. Tuck them under the next knot as well. You may have to use needle nose pliers to raise the knot enough. It also helps if you bend the bracelet. After the cord is tucked under, trim the cords and seal the ends with clear glue. To wear it, wrap it around your wrist and slip the knot through the loop.

Another Idea!

You can make a bracelet with two alternating colors. Ask an adult to join two cords together by burning each end with a lighter and then pressing them together with pliers. Then start the bracelet with the middle being the divide in the colors.

HEADBAND

You can make a beautiful headband to hold back your hair. Use any color ribbon or even several different colors to make your craft.

You'll Need

- ✔ Ribbon
- ✔ Scissors
- ✔ Ruler
- ✔ Thread
- ✔ Needle
- ✔ Bead
- ✔ Hard plastic headband

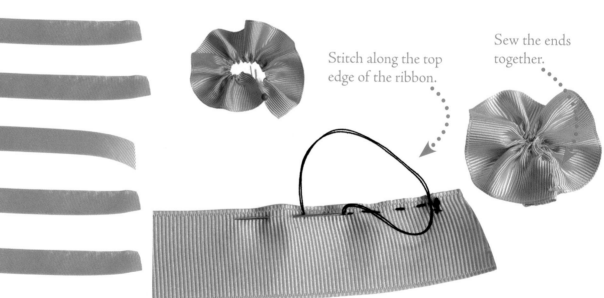

Stitch along the top edge of the ribbon.

Sew the ends together.

1 Cut five 6-inch (15 cm) pieces of pink ribbon. Cut five 12-inch (30 cm) pieces of thread. Thread the needle with the first thread and knot both ends together.

2 Starting at one end, stitch along the top edge of the ribbon. As you sew, pull to gather the ribbon. When you reach the end of the ribbon, gather it tightly and then cut the end of the thread and tie a knot.

3 Bring both edges of the ribbon together to make a circle. Using three stitches, sew the ends together.

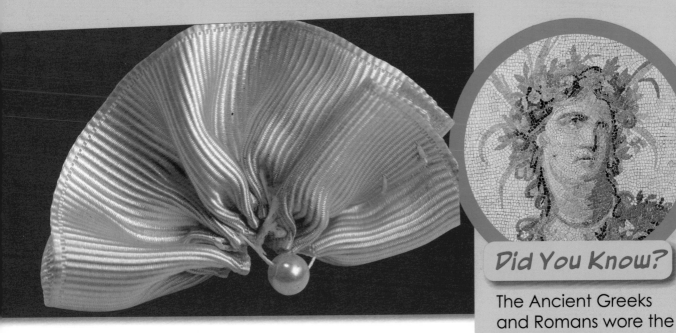

Did You Know?

The Ancient Greeks and Romans wore the first headbands, called hair wreaths, around 475 BCE. The wreaths were decorated with jewels made of gold and silver.

4 Thread the needle with another piece of thread. Starting from the back of the ribbon circle, push the needle through and through a bead. Take the needle back through the ribbon.

Sew the flower to the headband.

Another Idea!

To make layered flowers, repeat steps 1 to 3 with 4-inch and 2-inch (10 cm and 5 cm) pieces of ribbon. For step 4 take the needle through all three layers.

5 Sew the flower to the headband by looping around the headband several times. You could also glue it to the headband instead. Repeat this process until you have five flowers sewn on your hairband.

JEWELRY BOX

Now that you have made your jewelry, you need somewhere to store it. Make a beautiful jewelry box to keep your treasures!

You'll Need

- ✔ Box (new or reuse one)
- ✔ Paint
- ✔ Paintbrush
- ✔ Lids from used jars
- ✔ Scissors
- ✔ Tissue paper
- ✔ Decorative punch
- ✔ Glue
- ✔ Large bead

····· Glue

1 Paint your box. You may need to do this twice to cover the box completely. Use a jar lid to hold a small amount of paint.

2 Cut out shapes from tissue paper using scissors or a punch tool. Glue the shapes to the box. Cut a strip of paper to decorate the rim of the lid. Tuck the extra under the rim when you are gluing it on.

3 Make a handle by gluing tissue paper over a bead. Glue it to the top of your box.

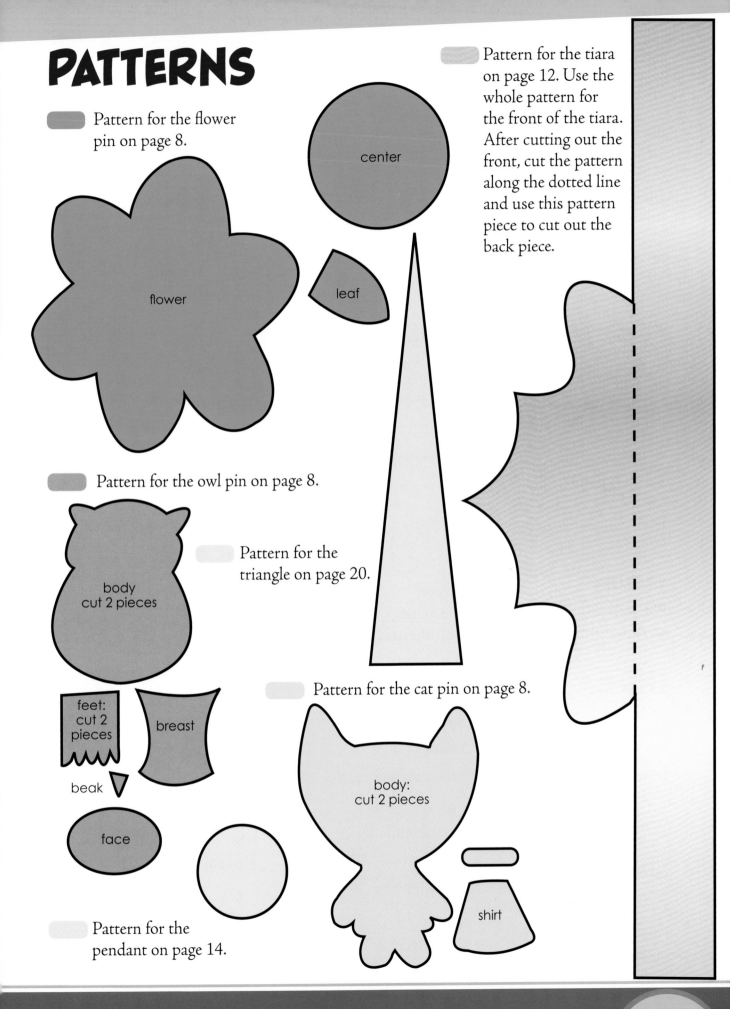

PATTERNS

Pattern for the flower pin on page 8.

flower

center

leaf

Pattern for the tiara on page 12. Use the whole pattern for the front of the tiara. After cutting out the front, cut the pattern along the dotted line and use this pattern piece to cut out the back piece.

Pattern for the owl pin on page 8.

body
cut 2 pieces

Pattern for the triangle on page 20.

feet:
cut 2
pieces

breast

beak

face

Pattern for the cat pin on page 8.

body:
cut 2 pieces

shirt

Pattern for the pendant on page 14.

31

GLOSSARY

accessory An item worn to complement an outfit.

carabiner A metal ring used in mountain climbing to hold rope.

jewel brad Jewels used for crafts with a metal tab at the back.

knead To work or mold something with the hands.

template A shape used as a pattern.

textile A type of cloth.

FOR MORE INFORMATION

FURTHER READING

Chorba, April. *Dot Jewelry: Make Pretty Paper Bracelets & Necklaces.* Palo Alto, CA: Klutz, 2013.

Cico Books. *My First Jewelry Making Book.* London, UK: CICO Books, 2013.

Nichols, Kaitlyn. *Make Clay Charms.* Palo Alto, CA: Klutz, 2013.

WEBSITES

For web resources related to the subject of this book, go to: **www.windmillbooks.com/weblinks** and select this book's title.

INDEX

B
barrette 22, 23
beads 5, 10, 14, 18, 20, 22, 24, 28, 30
bracelet 7, 10, 18, 19, 20, 24, 26, 27
buttons 24, 25

C
clay beads 10, 11
collage 7

F
felt pin 8, 9
friendship bracelet 18, 19

H
headband 28, 29

J
jewelry box 30

N
necklace 7, 10, 14, 15, 20

S
straw beads 20, 21

T
tiara 12, 13

W
washi tape 20, 21

Z
zipper pull 16, 17